A DOVE IN THE

GOLDEN

LIGHT

Betty,

Thank you for supporting "A Dove"

Continue to illuminate your light for the Kingdom.

Love, Peace, Love Faith & Joy

11/2023

A Dove In the Golden Light

"A Dove In the Golden Light" is dedicated to my loving husband Otis Lee Johnson; parents Adale and Sarah Clark; children Marquelle, Kendall and Kierra Johnson; deceased family members: Dearly beloved grandmother Charlotte Josephine McAllister, Aunt Annie McPherson, Uncle Thomas McAllister, Auntie Flora Mae McIver and Bonus Grandmother Lillie Mae Clark.

Shine on my Loves with your Golden Light!

"A Dove in the Golden Light" is a powerful work of literary art and I believe those who read it will be deeply moved, inspired and encouraged on their life journey, by the words shared. Alice poetically conveys the depth of her prayers, reflections and emotions in this spiritually charged book, empowering her readers to rest in the knowing that God is everything we know and believe him to be.

May the poems on these pages resonate in the hearts of its readers. Job well done, Alice!

Nia Sadé, The Literary Revolutionary

Publishing Partner

Preface

I believed that poetry is a means for me to express my inner being. Poetry gives me a unique sense of joy and compassion to interpret self-awareness. It is my passion that touches the core of my soul. Sharing unwavering faith which happens to be my truth.

The Light:

Beam, Bright, Cheerfulness, Energy, Exuberance, Friendliness, Happiness, Glow, Heat, Hotness, High Spiritedness, Illumination, Life, Liveliness, Luminosity Joy, Radiance, Spirit-filled, Temperateness, Shiny, Sunlit, Verve, Vivacity and Warmth.

WHO IS THE DOVE?

The Dove received comments that are favorable and unfavorable. Some of those comments developed my personality and traits. The Dove continues to illuminate in her darkest majestic moments. Below are a few comments she receives throughout her life:

Remember, words can elevate and diminish a soul. I recall the positive and negative to motivate my elevation to higher grounds.

The Dove: Metaphor

She has to be the center of attraction. She brightens the room. Exudes confidence. She has a sweet spirit. Always the same personality. She is warm. Always smiling. Loving attitude toward others. Why is she so nice all of the time? Oh, she is always doing something. She gives generously to help others. I love her smile. She cares for others' well-being. She has to be everywhere. Where does she get that energy? She is a glamour girl. She is always glowing. Stay home sometime, always making moves. Thanks for lifting my spirit today, young lady.

Well, I am that Dove that did not allow others to destroy my soul. God continues to shine on this Golden Dove in the Light.

Exploring, Learning and Living is my truth!!

THE DOVE IN THE GOLDEN LIGHT

A MAGNIFICENT DOVE GLIDE THROUGH THE CLOUDS,

LIMITLESS, EFFORTLESSLY DESCENDING

BEAUTIFUL WINGS OF WEIGHTLESS, WHITE SOFTNESS

AND EASE, YET STRONG AND POISED.

I STARE ABOVE AND AFAR, IN THE DISTANCE, THE SUN

LIGHTS THE WAY LIKE A SPARKLING

DIAMOND EXPOSED BRILLIANTLY AND MAJESTIC.

PEACE IS STILL, LOVING AND KIND;

THE SOFTNESS OF THE SUMMER BREEZE SENDING A WARM

MELODY OF THE LULLING COOS FROM

THE DOVE ABOVE WITH A SOUND SO PURE, SO MELLOW.

IT TUNES IN THE WHISTLING WIND, THE BRUSTLING
STREAM OF FRESH, CLEAR WATER MAKING A   PATH TO
NOWHERE, RUNNING FREE

QUIET YOUR MIND. LISTEN CAREFULLY, YOU WILL HEAR

STEPS AND WHISPERS OF HIS PRESENCE IN

THE MEADOWS OF BEAUTIFUL FLOWERS, COLORS OF THE

RAINBOW SHOWING PEACE AND PURITY OF LIFE

THE DOVE SYMBOLIZES THE TRUE PROMISE AND SWEET

ESSENCE OF THE GOLDEN LIGHT!!

Jesus is the Light of the World

The light that shines so bright to enhance mankind.

We were made to be in His image.

His light produces love, gratefulness and peace.

His light reigns from sea to shiny sea.

The light will beam from the beginning to the end.

Lighting projects from alpha to omega.

Jesus requires us to shine our light all day every day.

Your light provides generosity, peace, love and joy unconditionally.

Your light enhances favor in your life.

Jesus is the Light of the World.

Golden Light: I am the light of the world. Whoever follows me will never walk in darkness, but will have the light of life. (John 8:12)

Alice H. Johnson

De-Light Yourself

Stop; take a moment to turn on your light.

Hold up, you are still in the dark.

Let your light shine and give freely your heart.

Your light can help someone in despair.

Your light can produce hope, faith and wisdom to a man, woman, boy and girl!

Jesus is the light of the world.

We are images of God.

We must love each other as we love Christ.

Let your light shine.

Delight yourself in the Lord, and He shall give you the desires of your heart.

Golden Light: Delight yourself in the Lord, and he shall give you the desires of your heart. (Psalm 37:4)

The Golden Dove Image

The dove awaits to shine for peace, understanding and love.

Peace is found within the dove's wings.

No one will understand the dove's heart to have empathy for others.

The dove realizes God is shining a Golden Light to guide her path.

The dove will move forward in her destiny knowing she is never alone.

The dove follows her faith and will help others to gain theirs.

The dove stands alone and watches the hate and lies formed by others.

The dove will step back and allow others to think they are above all.

The dove will continue to praise God for His light that looks low and reaches high.

The dove prays to God to bring her truth and to ask for the Golden Light!

Be Bold, Be Loved, Be You

Be bold to stand up for what you believed to be your truth.

Be bold when displaying your compassion to others; know your circle of friends and family.

Believe in God.

You are His child.

He is your shepherd guiding his sheep.

Allow Him to guide you in your actions.

Pray and believe in His word.

Be loved, spread love and share love.

Be you, don't change to fit in.

Show your true colors and speak your mind.

You are uniquely and wonderfully made by Our Lord Jesus Christ!

Golden Light: "The fruit of the spirit is love, joy, peace, patience, kindness, generosity, faithfulness, and gentleness." (Gal. 5:22-23)

Savior

Lord, you are my crown and glory.

I thank you for your grace and mercy.

You have been my savior.

I cry for your unfailing powers.

My blessings overflow with your favor.

Just when I needed you the most!!

Lord, You may not come when I want You, but You are always on time.

I have been persecuted by the evil one.

However, Your unfailing love surrounded me and protected me.

When the evil one placed me in the snare.

Lord, You dropped a net and delivered me.

I thank You right now Lord!

Golden Light: " I, even I, am the LORD, And there is no savior besides Me". (Isaiah 43:11)

Alice H. Johnson

My Joy

God, you are my joy!

You touch the pivoting points in my bones.

My happiness is from You.

Many times, I sing joy from my soul.

This is the joy that I feel within my heart.

Your spirit is within me.

I am counting it all Joy.

For you are our glory and joy.

My discomforts, sadness, disappointments, loss, betrayal, and pain.

It's rewarding to me knowing that deep in my heart, you will be my peace and my Joy.

Holy Spirit, You abound in hope.

Thank You for shining your light and sparkling Joy in my heart.

Lord, You are my Joy!

Golden light: "Those who sow in tears shall reap with shouts in joy!." (Psalm 124:5)

Thankfulness

Thank You Lord for lifting my doubts and having the power to reign supreme control over my life.

I can always depend on Your hand to bring me out. You have been there for me time and time again. Thank You for your mercy Lord.

I have been in darkness and it was You who brought me into the light. I will not turn back to the darkness.

Thanks be to God who giveth me the victory through our Lord Jesus Christ. What a delightful-giving God we serve.

You are so awesome and generous Lord. I will continue to praise your name.

Golden Light: " Then your light shall break forth like the dawn, and your healing shall spring up quickly". (Isaiah 58:8)

Belief

Lord, I believe you will never leave me nor forsake me.

I walked in darkness and you cared for me.

I have been thirsty.

You provided ever-lasting water.

I have been in the pits.

You picked me up and gave me the grace and strength to carry on.

I believe in You Lord.

Your power is immeasurable.

You have provided resolution in the darkest times.

I believe in You my Lord.

I have faith in You Lord.

I will call on You Lord for deliverance.

Your light is the source of energy I need.

Alice H. Johnson

I will worship You in spirit and in truth.

I will place my belief and hope in You my Lord!

Golden Light: "Then Jesus declared, "I am the bread of life. Whoever comes to me will never go hungry and whoever believes in me will never be thirsty". (John 6:35)

Dear Momma

I love and care so much about you.

You taught me to pray and bow down each and every day.

I listened to your words.

Yes, I did.

I am practicing my faith and trusting in the will of the Lord.

Thank you Momma for teaching and modeling these values in my heart.

Mom, I remembered you said, "pray Alice, trust and believe in Jesus' name".

The light of the Lord is unwavering through my trust and belief in His Holy and divine power.

His loving water flows freely through the core of my soul.

Golden Light: "Whoever believes in me, as scriptures has said, rivers of living water will flow from within them". (John 7:38)

Precious Father

I get so much joy when I think about You.

I feel a special way when I hear Your name.

You said in Your word that You will never leave me nor forsake me.

Precious father!!

Thank You Jesus for your words of power.

I will trust and believe in Your spirit every hour.

Precious Father!

The opportunity for experiences is limitless.

I find deep internal potential.

The light shines with abundant love.

It glows, glows and glows.

Blessings radiate my soul within.

Golden Light: Praise the Lord, O my soul; and all that is wthin me, Bless his holy name". (Psalm 103:1)

You Are My Strength

As I sit here all alone in this chair,

Who shall I call?

Is there someone who wants to share some time with me?

I don't know!!

It's very sad to say!!

Yes, I thought I had a friend that would forever come my way!!

My friend is here, Jesus!!

He was here all along.

What was I thinking?

I do know He will never leave nor forsake me.

Just sitting alone and thankful for my rock, shield, protector, provider and loving friend.

He cares about me and all that I am going through.

Lord, you are my love and strength!!

Alice H. Johnson

Golden Light: God is the strength of my heart and my portion forever". (Psalm 73:26)

Transformation Prayer

Our Father, whom art in heaven.

Lord, keep me in Your perfect peace.

How I love Your precious name.

Bless me Lord.

Strengthen my faith.

Guide me to move from doubt to belief.

Lord, when I was down and out in despair,

I know my Father, You were always there.

Deliver me with Your omnipresent power.

Just transform me Lord; take me higher and higher.

I need to see Your light.

Shine on me Lord.

Shine, Shine, Shine!!

Shine, Shine, Shine!!

Alice H. Johnson

Amen

Golden Light: "Humble yourselves before the Lord and he will lift you up". (James 4:10)

Lift the Lord Higher

I feel blessed to have a wonderful Father that shines His light on me.

Oh Lord, thank You for providing me with all my needs and desires.

Oh Lord, there is none like You.

I will praise Your name and lift you higher Lord!!

You said in Your word, "delight yourself in me and I will give you the desires of your heart".

I will lift you higher in the good times and the bad times.

Your name will reign forever in my heart.

I will seek your face and lift you higher my Lord!

Golden Light: " I will instruct you and teach you the way you should go". (Psalm 32:8)

Sister

Walk with your head high to the sky.

Walk proud and swing those arms as if you own the Nile.

Walk on with your bad self and drink from the fountain of love.

Walk tall, the light is shining and illuminating your inner spirit.

You are amazing, brilliant, charismatic, and compassionate to help others.

Hold on to that spirit my Sister.

Grace your humbleness with spirit and truth.

You are a winner my Sister.

Remember the Lord our Father is judging you.

Golden Light: "Humble yourselves, therefore, under God's mighty hand, that he may lift you up in due time". (1 Peter 5:6)

Pray On

Be what you want to be.

Have faith in our Father.

Oh yes, that's me!

I pray for justice.

I pray for peace.

I endure pain on a daily basis.

Watching out for uncaring and blatant racist.

Pray on my sister and brother too.

What my God has done for others, He will do for you!!

Pray on!!

Pray on!!

Pray on!!

There will be a brighter day!!

Pray on Pray on Pray on Pray on

Alice H. Johnson

I say!!

Golden Light: Rejoice always, pray without ceasing.
(1 Thessalonians 5:16)

The Precious Little Ones

His little babies are vessels of peace.

Oh, Mommy loves her babies.

They have a mind of their own.

Curious and intelligent, yes they are.

I know we needed to pray for their continued growth.

It is assuring to know our God is watching His children.

Thank You Lord so much for Your sovereign powers.

We appreciate You Lord for Your precious gifts.

I am teaching them to always lean on You Father to seek wisdom in their life.

Thank You Lord so much for shining Your light.

Modeling love and peace to move forward in their daily life.

You are the Savior of the World!!

Offering protection to the meek and weary.

Alice H. Johnson

Thank You Lord, so very much for gleaming your love to the world.

I will always give you the glory and look to the hills whence cometh my help. The radiant light that illuminates my soul, knowing and feeling that Jesus loves His little children.

Golden Light: Jesus said, "Let the little children come to me, and forbid them not, to come unto me: for of such is the kingdom of heaven" (Matthew 19:14)

My Son

Listen to your parents, we will tell you what is right.

If not, you will find yourself lost in the middle of the night.

Put your head on straight, study hard.

So that you are not the one to learn too late.

We love you son and are so proud of your life.

You are our hero.

God has been with you through so much!

Keep yourself together, stay focused, pray and always trust God!

My son, it is you, who He is shining your light and providing love.

Yes, it is you!!

Golden Light: " Train up a child in the way he should go, And when he is old, he will not depart from it". (Proverbs 22:6)

Protection Spiritual Warfare

Put on the whole armor of God for your protection.

For we wrestle not against flesh and blood, but against principalities, against powers, against the rulers of the darkness of the world, against spiritual wickedness in high places.

Wherefore take unto you the whole armor of God, which ye may be able to withstand in the evil day and having done all to stand.

Stand therefore, having your loins girt about with truth, and having on the breastplate of righteousness.

Golden Light: "Finally, be strong in the Lord and in his mighty power". (Ephesians 6:11)

Call Him

Our God is awesome!

His love abounds to all.

Give Him a prayer and a call.

There are no barriers to His love, it endures forever and ever.

Rich or poor, sick or well, black or white.

Call on His Holy name.

He is waiting for you to seek His face.

Praise Him in the dark or light.

He will be there for you.

His awesome wisdom endures forever.

Rich or poor, sick or well, black or white.

Call on His Holy name.

Call on Him, trust Him and He will come through as pure gold.

Golden Light: "At that time people began to call upon the name of the Lord". (Genesis 4:26)

Faithfulness

My trust and faith grow and grow to bring new life.

Great is Thy faithfulness.

God's faithfulness is not our faithfulness.

Having the faith of a mustard seed is all our Father requires.

But, without Faith, it is impossible to please Him; for he that cometh to God must believe that He is, and that He is the rewarder of them that diligently seek Him.

I pray daily for my faith and to irradiate the doubt that slips in like a serpent.

The daily woes that lurk to steal, kill and destroy my belief that God is omnipresent, He is my comfort and strength. He is reliable, steadfast and unwavering.

Oh, what peace I have relying on His faithfulness. Selah

Golden Light: "The promises He made still hold true because He does not change". (Malachi 3:6)

Choose Love

Look at that smile on your beautiful face.

The gleam in your eyes.

The tone of your skin.

Beauty expands because of the love you exude inside and out.

You are fearfully and wonderfully made.

Marvelous are Your works, and that my soul knows very well.

You provide encouragement, care for others for no particular reason.

Girl, keep it moving.

Love God and others as you love yourself.

I am with you always, to the very end of age, my endless lover.

Love is the fruit that continues to keep you strong and free.

Golden Light: "I praise you because I am fearfully and wonderfully made; your works are wonderful, I know that full well". (Psalm 139:14)

Friends

You are my friend.

We share the bond that ties our memories.

We have laughed, cried, sang and danced to life.

We started out wishing we had more. Through God's grace and mercy, we obtained more than we could have ever dreamed.

I love you my friend.

We don't communicate every day.

But, just like stars in the sky,

I know you are shining bright in your world.

Keep your spirit sweet and your heart straight on thee.

He will give you my friend, the desires of your heart.

Golden Light: "One who has unreliable friends soon comes to ruin, but there is a friend who sticks closer than a brother". (Proverbs 18:24)

Humble Soul

Humble yourself, remain peaceful. Use your discernment of others.

Understand when others are not with you.

You do not have to connect with everyone.

Humble Soul;

Starve the ego and feed the soul.

Humble yourself and never ever treat others as if they are less than you.

Continue to care for others and not try to rule over them. Humble soul;

Pride leads to disgrace but with humility comes wisdom.

Humble Soul;

Remain positive in negative situations.

He knows your heart, soul and mind.

Do not entertain a fool.

Alice H. Johnson

You cannot argue with a folly.

Speak peace, walk away, and pray. Humble soul.

Golden Light: "Whosever exalts himself will be humbled, and whoever humbles himself will be exalted". (Matthew 23:12)

Secrets

My Lord knows my secrets.

Some sweet and some bitter.

It doesn't matter, I can depend on the Lord to guide and hold on to my truth.

I am not judged nor compared by others when it comes to my secret keeper.

He knows and comprehends all of my issues, concerns and problems.

I cannot hide anything from thee, my skeleton bones in the closet.

Thank You Lord for not sharing, comparing, or judging me.

You hold my confidence, mysteries and enigmas.

Cultivate a secret life with Christ.

He is waiting on you.

Golden Light: " This will take place on the day when God judges people's secret through Jesus Christ, as my gospel declares". (Romans 2:16)

The Gift

Have you received the gift?

What gift you may ask?

I am speaking of the gift of love.

Yes, you have been given so many opportunities to share the gift.

Oh, you didn't know.

You will reap exactly what you sow.

Karma!

Share love, bring love, speak love and watch your universe accept love.

Share love, bring love, speak love and watch your universe accept love.

Bring it into your existence.

Create your universe, atmosphere, and environment.

Then you shall receive.

You will be so thrilled that you opened your heart to the gift.

Golden Light: "Be not deceived; God is not mocked: for whatsoever a man soweth, that shall he also reap". (Galatians 6:7)

Mercy

Have mercy on me dear Lord.

I thank You for spreading Your mercies, compassion, and having pity on me.

You Lord have protected me from harms that were seen and unseen.

I am crying tears of joy because I know within my heart that Your mercies endure forever.

Your understanding and benevolence secure my heart.

My blessings overflow.

Kindness and godsend angels encamp my environment.

I am depending on You!

Thank You Lord for Your continued mercy and grace.

Golden Light: "Be merciful to me." For I cry to You all day long". (Psalm 86)

Power Lord

Who has the almighty power that controls all?

Your unwavering power prevails from alpha to omega.

The beginning and the end.

There is power in the name of Jesus that is unbendable, unfaltering, unshakable, firm and steady.

There is no divine power that will ever compare to You!!

I trust and believe in Your power Lord.

You can do all things!

Your power is the force that spoke everything into existence.

Whatever God speaks for you to do,

He will give you the matter to see it through!

Golden Light: "But Jesus looked at them and said, "with man this is impossible, but with God all things are possible". (Matthew 19:26)

Intercession Prayer

I saw you crying in that chair waiting to hear the good news.

You have waited so long and time seems to pass slowly.

You cast all of your cares in thee and so have I!!

Sometimes your desire can be one prayer away.

Do not give up my brother and sister, continue to uphold your faith.

We shall pray together for one another.

At all times.

I will pray to Thee.

I am praying without ceasing in spirit and truth.

Which includes my enemies and those that persecute me.

Yes, my Lord Blesses me! Thank you, my friend.

I am giving thanks to the Lord, for He is good.

He is constantly making a way out of no way.

Oh, so don't get it twisted, I am highly favored by my Father.

He gives me more than I can ever repay.

Golden Light: " But I say to you, love your enemies and pray for those who persecute you"! (Matthew 5:44-45)

Patience

How long Lord must I wait?

I have been waiting so long Lord.

Help me to be patient and remain in your will.

I am resting in Your loving arms for I know you have plans for me; to bring hope so that I may prosper.

I am leaning on Your everlasting arm Father.

Patience is better than strength.

I know my Father God that everything cannot be rushed.

For You will deliver my need in Your own timing in Your own way.

In advance, I thank You Lord!!

Golden Light: "Be still, and know that I am God, I will be exalted among the nations, I will be exalted in the earth!" (Psalm 46:11)

Trusting

I am trusting You with all my heart and no longer depending on my own understanding, Lord.

I am trusting Your will to be done.

Every day and every hour, I am trusting!!

I am placing all my hope and wisdom in You.

Lord, my trust in You has been my stronghold.

I will trust in You for my salvation, my fortress, my refuge, oh yes, my deliverer.

In the days of darkness, depression, pain, sickness, and weakness, it was You that brought me through!

You are my protector from the evil one.

You saved me from the ones that persecute.

Lord, You are my hope.

My hope is placed in thee.

I will not waver nor turn around because God is always faithful to bring me through.

Alice H. Johnson

Golden Light: Trust in the Lord with all your heart and lean not on your own understanding; in all your ways submit to him, and he will make your paths straight. (Proverbs 3:5-6)

I Hear the Music

I hear ringing sweet melodies in my heart.

I love the tune as it harmonizes something that played days gone.

I hear the music with so much grace; it is so compelling for me to thank God.

The music is enchanting to the mercy that has confined me to be in his presence.

I will rather be in no other place than to listen to music that transforms multiple words of wisdom and truth.

The music is a treasure that has placed my belief on a higher level.

I am listening to the beat of my song in my heart.

It is playing at the right time and linking me to my higher power.

Only the music for me can take me to a peaceful zone within my limitless space.

God, you are so amazing!!

Golden Light: "Sing to him, sing praises to him, tell of all his wonderful acts". (Psalm 105:2)

My Dear and Loving Mother

I bid much love and happiness to you my mother.

Your kindness to others is so prevalent and embodies your total essence within.

Your words are felt with peace.

Tranquility is mobilizing throughout my soul when you step into my space.

I honor and love you for being there with me in my darkest and happiest moments.

I can truly say, I love you much more.

I am blessed.

Thank You my Lord and Savior for my dear mother.

Golden Light: "Children obey your parents in the Lord because this is right. Honor your father and your mother, which is the first commandment with a promise- that it may go well with you and you may have a long life." (Ephesians 6: 1-3)

Simple Girl Standing In the Light

Who are you over there?

Yes, I see you in the light.

Your love to help others.

The smiles you give are a beacon of hope to most.

Simple girl, love yourself and continue to

exude joy.

Stay strong in the Lord.

Honor the light!

Who are you over there?

Yes, I see you in the light.

Your love to help others.

The smiles you give are a beacon of hope to most.

Simple girl, love yourself and continue to exude joy.

Stay strong in the Lord and read the word.

Alice H. Johnson

Stand up for yourself in today's woe.

Remind yourself that creativity designs your mold.

Simple girl, your brown eyes share gleam and splendid memories of what you are going through.

Simple girl, your faith will bring you through the most important times and experiences of your life.

Simple girl, trust God!!

Simple girl, trust God, shine your light.

Golden Light: Thy word is a lamp unto my feet, and a light unto my path. (Psalm 119:105)

Express Yourself

You have such beautiful skin.

The mocha, caramel, honey glow, mahogany, latte, beige, coffee, brown sugar, and ivory.

I can go on and on.

The skin of royalty, power and sustained beauty.

You can do whatever you set on your mind.

Determination, perseverance, prayer and fasting are the tools for developing yourself.

Love yourself and express the power of divine grace and mercy to others.

Share peace, smile, sing and be joyful with others.

Speak positively and look into the eyes of others.

Fret not thyself of evil-doers.

Do the right thing!

Golden Light: "Fret not thyself of evildoers, neither be envious against the workers of iniquity. For they shall be cut down like the grass, and wither as the green herb.. .Rest in the Lord, and wait patiently for him; fret not thyself because of him who prospereth in his way". (Psalm 37: 1-4)

Goodnight Love

I had the most amazing day with you.

You allowed me to feel so wonderful.

I was uniquely created by you.

I absorbed the fresh air and the beautiful flowers you sent to me.

I was able to touch and smell the roses you provided for me today.

Just for me!

I am so content with you.

You have given me all that I ever needed.

I am singing myself to sleep.

I am praying that others will get the opportunity to open their hearts to feel your presence.

That they will learn to follow you!

I am committed to you.

For, I will never give up hope and stop praising You my Lord.

Alice H. Johnson

Good night love.

Golden Light: "The Lord is my Shepherd, I shall not want" (Psalm 23:1)

Anointed Grace

She feels the spirit of the Lord in her life.

Her spouse is working on his faith and showing his precious bride honor and love.

The children are preserving their life and helping others to grow stronger in their faith in God.

The job that she attends offers support and guidance while accepting Christ in spirit and truth.

The friends that she meets and greets provide peace and joy. Know your circle of anointed grace and accept the gift of life God has for you.

Pray to God for wisdom, love and truth.

Anointed Grace, you are uniquely and wonderfully made.

He designed you to accept His word and believe that He died on the cross for your salvation.

Anointed Grace, believe in the power in the blood of God!

Golden Light: But you have an anointing from the Holy One, and all of you know the truth. (1 John 2:20)

Family Love

Togetherness, kinfolk, loved ones, lineage, and bloodline brings family love.

The family has various levels of love to meet each other's needs.

When the family joins together, there is so much love to engage each other.

Oh, it is working to provide love to kinfolk because of what we go through in life.

Loved ones know the hurt and pain that can cause each of us to change our thoughts and beliefs.

Try not to displace your sadness, anxiety and fears on your family lineage.

Begin a new pattern of thought and discuss past stressors with the family.

Create your own family's legacy.

Hope for the best to give love and pray to gain your family's love.

Golden Light: "We love because he first loved us" (1 John 4:19)

Purposely Growing

Be proud of who you are.

Know for yourself that you are living today for a purpose and on purpose.

No one can ever take your place in life.

Seek and you shall find what your purpose is in this life's cycle.

When your purpose is discovered, nurture your mind, body and soul for peace, love and understanding.

Continue to protect your growth pattern from negative attitudes and nay-sayers, imbue your environment.

Retain positive experiences, people and places for your growth purposefully.

We all must learn to discern those that are for us and those that use and abuse.

Pay close attention to those that no longer need or value your worth.

Watch and pray for them, then move on!

Golden Light: " So rid yourself of all malice, all deceit, all hypocrisy, envy and all slander. Like newborn infants, desire the pure spiritual milk, so that you may grow by it for your salvation since you have tasted that Lord is good". (1 Peter 2:1-3)

Knowledge

Reading and listening to the word enhances your knowledge base.

Understanding the word brings peace in the most chaotic situations.

Understanding the word brings comfort in the time of a great loss.

Understanding the word protects when the devil attempts to steal, kill and destroy.

Understanding the word brings faith when doubt ensues.

Understanding the word brings trust when hope is lost.

Understanding the word is an ongoing process that will take you to higher ground when you forsake evil and ask forgiveness.

Golden Light: The Spirit of the Lord, will rest on him. The spirit of wisdom and of understanding, the Spirit of counsel and of might, the Spirit of knowledge and fear of the Lord." (Isaiah 11:2)

Alice H. Johnson

Bag People

I see you carrying that load.

A bag full of lies,

A bag full of shame.

A bag full of hurt.

A bag full of depression.

A bag full of stress.

A bag full of anxiety.

You walk around crying inside and smiling on the outside.

We hear your lies.

We see your shame.

We feel your pain.

You try to conceal your emotions.

We see your bags!

They are transparent.

We want you to drop off each of those bags.

You have been repressing and suppressing your problems for too long.

Bring your feelings to the surface. Lay those bags down.

Clear your mind and leave those bags right here!

Golden Light: Cast your cares on the LORD and he will sustain you; he will never let the righteous be shaken". (Psalm 55:22)

Encouraging Thoughts:

Always give thanks to the Lord, for He is good.

He is constantly making a way out of no way.

Oh, so don't get it twisted, I am highly favored by my father.

He gives me more than I can ever repay.

When I think of the goodness of the LORD and all that He has done for me, my soul just cries out!

He provides peace beyond peace!

Love beyond Love!

Joy beyond Joy!

Grace beyond Grace!

Mercy beyond Mercy!

The light is shining brightly!

Worship him in love and truth to obtain the light!

Conflict and trouble do not last forever!

Get out of the darkness!

Stop letting your past dictate your future!

Shine your light!

Give it to God and rest!

Walk into your divine destiny!

God is ever faithful!

Golden Light: The humble will see their God at work and be glad. Let all who seek God's help be encouraged. (Psalm 62:32)

Alice H. Johnson

Humble Soul

Humble yourself, remain peaceful.

Use your discernment of others.

Understand when others are not with you.

You do not have to connect with everyone.

Humble Soul;

Starve the ego and feed the soul.

Humble yourself and never ever treat others as if they are less than you.

Continue to care for others and not rule over them.

Humble soul;

Pride leads to disgrace but with humility comes wisdom.

Humble Soul;

Remain positive in negative situations.

He knows your heart, soul and mind.

Do not entertain a fool.

You cannot argue with a folly.

Speak peace, walk away, and pray.

Humble soul.

Golden Light: Though the Lord is great, he cares for the humble, but he keeps his distance from the proud. (Psalm 138:6)

Kindness

You are my protection!

You want me to be healed and whole.

Your guidance for me is to treat others with kindness, love, dignity and respect.

The guidance you have instilled in my heart is to gain understanding.

Exude kindness, generosity and being non-judgemental to others.

I must rest in your word and believe that there is nothing too hard for You Lord.

Your kindness prevails in my thoughts.

Your word is quite clear, though he falls, he shall not be utterly cast down for the Lord upholdeth him with His hand!

I know that You are the creator of all.

Father, you are the alpha and omega.

The beginning and the end.

Golden Light: Discover for yourself that the Lord is kind. Come to him for protection and you will be glad.

Longsuffering Patience

I have been waiting so long for that peace.

I am praying for that peace.

Laughing internally knowing and understanding that at that peace, everyone is not happy for me.

They manipulated me through mind games, power, and persecution.

So you have your imps. I have Jesus.

You have letters. I have Jesus.

You have powers in high places. I have Jesus.

He places me at peace.

Leave me in my peace.

He is walking with me in that peace, in the midst of our storms.

Pray with me in that peace.

Jesus will calm my storm and yours also.

Thankfully, He is always with us.

Alice H. Johnson

We are never ever alone.

Peace be still.

Golden Light: "Peace be still". And the wind ceased, and there was a great storm. (Matthew 8:23-27)

SHINE YOUR LIGHT Daily:

How does your light shine?

What are you doing to seek the glow of love?

The brighter your light, the more you will feel that you are no longer in darkness!

You are free to illuminate your path!

Luminosity produces your radiance to shine!

The recipe to obtain light is in you!

Beam while in fear, pain, hurt, despair, sadness, isolation and depression!

Keep your faith strong and pray for joy to come to your heart! People can be very mean and salty.

The Dove in the Golden Light:

Is the Light of love, gratefulness, peace, truth, and humbleness. In the event you don't know or understand, trust your Light. I knew in my darkest days, I would soon be subjected to the Light. My trust is in the Light.

The Lord will deliver your path. Joy, peace and love will come. During the worst periods of your life, you will need an anchor to hold on to. You will need a friend closer than your brother or sister. You will need to share your deepest dreams, problems, secrets, mistakes and sorrows. You will need help with addictions, depression, anxiety stress, grief and growth. I Trusted and Believed in his word to bring me to the Light!

Joy, Peace, gratefulness, love, and humility illuminate your Light!!!!

Alice H. Johnson

SHINE YOUR LIGHT.

IT IS YOUR TIME.

BEAM INTENTIONALLY AND ON PURPOSE.

Define your Light: Focus on you. Self-care. Your environment can determine how you feel and shine your light. Cultivate positivity in your space. Nurture your environment to ensure your light will illuminate.

Beam

Cheerfulness

Energy

Exuberance

Friendliness

Forgiveness

Happiness

Generous

Gratefulness

Glow

Heat

High Spirtitfulness

Alice H. Johnson

Humility

Illumination Life

Kindness

Love

Liveliness

Luminosity Joy

Peace

Radiance

Temperateness Shiny Sunlit

Verve

Vivacity

Warmth

Steps to define your Darkness daily to discover your Light. To overcome the darkness. Declutter toxic spirits from destroying your Light. What's stopping you from shining your Light? Seek and you shall find.

Anger

Anxiousness

Bitterness

Cruelness

Depressive

Despair

Evilness

Fearful

Frustrated

Hatred

Isolation

Jealousy

Malice

Meanness

Mischieviousness

Nastiness

Nervousness

Spiteful

Stressful

ABOUT THE AUTHOR

Alice Johnson and her husband live in the Augusta, Georgia area. She is a native of Fayetteville, NC. She earned her Master's Degree at the University of South Carolina, Columbia and graduated from Saint Augustine's College (University) with a bachelor's degree in Criminal Justice. She is a practicing licensed Social Worker, ACSW, CCTP, psychotherapist, Crisis Interventionist, and Mental Health Keynote Speaker. Alice Johnson also received recognition from the Charlie Norwood Veterans Affairs Medical Center Director's Office, "Making a Difference Award FY 2022", providing our nation's heroes with their Mental Health treatment and psychosocial needs. Alice enjoys spending quality time with her family and friends, worshipping and being an active member in her church, listening to inspirational music, reading, dancing, physical fitness, nature, traveling abroad and domestic, fashion, public speaking, vintage shopping and creative art.

Alice H. Johnson

Alice H. Johnson

_____

_____

_____

_____

_____

_____

_____

_____

_____

_____

_____

_____

_____

_____

_____

_____

_____

_____

Alice H. Johnson

43414276R00049